JB JOSSEY-BASS

THE MOST EXTREME PREDATORS

Animal Planet

By Mary Packard

Foreword by Kevin Mohs and Ian McGee

BICENTENNIAL
1807
WILEY
2007
BICENTENNIAL

John Wiley & Sons, Inc.

©2007 Discovery Communications, Inc. Animal Planet, Animal Planet ROAR Reach Out. Act. Respond., The Most Extreme, and related logos and indicia are trademarks of Discovery Communications, Inc., used under license. All rights reserved.

Published by Jossey-Bass
A Wiley Imprint
989 Market Street, San Francisco, CA 94103-1741
www.josseybass.com

Developed by Nancy Hall, Inc.
Photo research by Linda Falken
Designed by Alisa Komsky and Tom Koken
Cover design by Alisa Komsky

DCI Book Development Team:
Maureen Smith, Executive Vice President & General Manager, Animal Planet
Kevin Mohs, Vice President, Animal Genre, Discovery US Networks Production
Peggy Ang, Vice President, Animal Planet Marketing
Ian McGee, Series Producer, National History New Zealand
Carol LeBlanc, Vice President, Licensing
Elizabeth Bakacs, Vice President, Creative Services
Caitlin Erb, Licensing Specialist

Jossey-Bass books and products are available through most bookstores. To contact Jossey-Bass directly, call our Customer Care Department within the U.S. at 800-956-7739, outside the U.S. at 317-572-3986, or fax 317-572-4002.

Jossey-Bass also publishes its books in a variety of electronic formats. Some content that appears in print may not be available in electronic books.

Library of Congress Cataloging-in-Publication Data

Packard, Mary.
  Animal Planet : The most extreme predators / by Mary Packard ; foreword by Kevin Mohs and Ian McGee. — 1st ed.
    p. cm.
  Includes index.
  ISBN: 978-0-7879-8664-3 (cloth)
  1. Predatory animals—Juvenile literature. 2. Animal locomotion—Juvenile literature. I. Title.
  QL758.P33 2007
  591.5'3—dc22
                              2006038511

Printed in China
First edition

10 9 8 7 6 5 4 3 2 1

REACH OUT. ACT. RESPOND.
Go to AnimalPlanet.com/ROAR and find out how you can be a voice for animals everywhere!

TABLE of CONTENTS

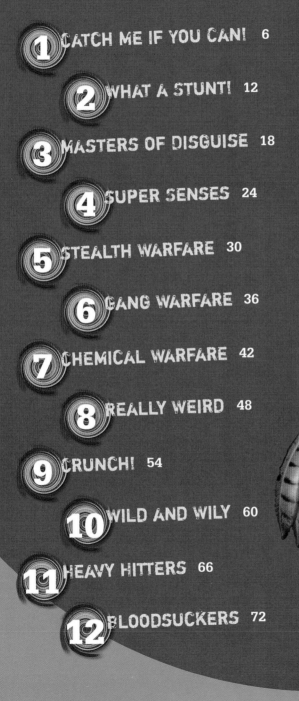

Foreword

To me, countdown shows are addictive, because I feel compelled to watch until the very end to discover who or what ranks number one in a given category—even if it's dance moves that changed the world. Given that and my knowledge of animals, it's not surprising that I decided to propose a countdown series about the most amazing behaviors and abilities of all kinds of creatures to Animal Planet. The network liked the idea, so I teamed up with Ian McGee, an entomologist turned television producer for Natural History New Zealand, who once measured caterpillar heads for a living—and *The Most Extreme* was born.

To make the series fun and interactive as well as informative, Ian and I made sure that each show had a unique ranking system that allowed us to include some of the world's wildest animal behavior. That's how some tiny ants landed in the #2 spot in our "Weird Weapons" episode (Amazonian ants build a fungus framework filled with tiny holes where they hide to ambush larger bugs!).

Animal Planet The Most Extreme books follow the same format as the show and are filled with offbeat facts about animals and the astonishing things they do—such as deep-sea anglerfish, which have a built-in glow-in-the-dark lure to attract prey; and ant lion larvae, which dig a steep, sandy pit and then bury themselves at the bottom and wait for prey to fall into the trap.

Ian, the production team, and I all share a passion for animals, so *The Most Extreme* series has been a filmmaker's dream come true, and we are delighted that there are now books based on the series. If, after watching the show or reading the books, you find yourself sharing unusual animal facts or debating the selections in a *Most Extreme* countdown with friends or family, then Ian and I feel that we have succeeded, because we've not only entertained you, but also engaged you in the extraordinary natural world that surrounds you. So get ready to take reading to the *Most Extreme* as you delve into the pages of *The Most Extreme Predators*, a totally awesome book.

Sincerely,

Kevin Mohs

Executive Producer for Animal Planet

Ian McGee

Series Producer for
Natural History New Zealand

Predators in the News!

The animal kingdom can seem cruel and unfair, as these headlines attest. But predators don't kill for sport (as some humans do), they hunt to survive. And while all predators do this by preying on other animals—some do it in a more extreme manner than others.

In this book you'll meet all kinds of predators. Some rely on speed or acrobatic high jinks to catch prey. Others are wilier, donning disguises or using their smarts or their senses to trap unsuspecting prey. For other predators, hunting cooperatively or using chemical warfare is the way to go.

Whatever their method for catching their next meal, all the predators gathered in this book are the most extreme of their kind. In a kill-or-be-killed world, these animals reign supreme.

CHAPTER 1
CATCH ME IF YOU CAN!

Speed is enormously important to a predator, especially at mealtime. Why? If a predator doesn't move fast enough, its dinner just might escape. Put on your running shoes and get ready to meet ten extremely speedy predators.

#9
Wind Scorpion

Actually, the wind scorpion is not a scorpion but another kind of arachnid. Compared to its spider relatives, it does seem to move as fast as the wind, though, reaching speeds of up to 10 miles per hour. Its legs end in sticky suction cup–like suckers that make it easy for the wind scorpion to climb and hold onto prey. Wind scorpions can be found in the dry areas of most parts of the world.

#10
Australian Tiger Beetles

The world's fastest-running insects are Australian tiger beetles. In hot pursuit of spiders and insects such as flies, ants, and grasshoppers, one species runs at a rate of 5 miles per hour. That may not sound very fast, but in human terms it would equal more than 338 miles per hour! There's only one problem: The beetles have to keep stopping to make sure they're going the right way because their eyes can't refocus fast enough to keep up with their running speed!

Black Mamba

The black mamba of Africa is the fastest snake around. It can reach top speeds of 10 to 12 miles per hour in short bursts over level ground. When hunting small animals, a black mamba delivers one bite to the neck and waits for its venom to take effect. Only two drops of this highly toxic venom can kill a human.

I should have worn my sneakers.

#7

Six-lined Racerunner

Six stripes run from the back of the six-lined racerunner's head to the base of its tail. That and the fact that at 18 miles per hour, it's the world's fastest-running lizard are what give this North American reptile its name. The six-lined racerunner is highly active, even during the day when other lizards are snoozing.

#6

Gentoo Penguin

Looking a lot like a speedy little torpedo, a gentoo penguin speeds along at just over 20 miles per hour in pursuit of prey such as squid and cod in the icy seas around Antarctica. That makes it the fastest swimming bird in the world. This penguin catches most of its prey close to the surface but is known to dive as deep as 330 feet. When it walks on land, its long tail feathers stick out behind it.

Gentoo penguins often hunt in groups, called rafts, of several hundred.

THAT'S WILD!

#5 Shortfin Mako Shark

The shortfin mako shark has been known to swim faster than 22 miles per hour in short bursts, making it the world's fastest shark. It's a pretty amazing jumper, too, leaping as high as 20 feet out of the water. Found in warmer seas around the world, it averages 5 to 8 feet long but can grow as long as 12 feet and weigh as much as 1,000 pounds. This shark prefers fish such as herring, mackerel, tuna, and swordfish, but sometimes eats porpoises and sea turtles. Its long, sharp teeth come in handy when hanging onto slippery prey.

#4 California Sea Lion

Easily reaching speeds of up to 25 miles per hour, California sea lions are the fastest pinnipeds (a family of meat-eating sea mammals that includes seals and walruses) in the ocean. They can dive up to 240 feet deep in pursuit of squid, octopi, rockfish, and the many other sea creatures they like to eat.

On land, California sea lions use their large back flippers to help them move about. Noisy and social, they often gather in large groups at favorite resting places, like Pier 39 in San Francisco, California, where they've been entertaining tourists since 1990. Many of the trained "seals" you can see in zoos or aquariums are actually the smart and playful California sea lions.

That sun sure feels good.

At up to 1,000 pounds, male California sea lions are about 4.5 times as big as females.

THAT'S WILD!

8

Dragonfly

There have been dragonflies on Earth for as long as 250 million years. One fossil of a dragonfly dating back to that time has a two-foot wingspan. Today's dragonflies are not that big, but they are still efficient predators. In a high-speed chase, it's not unusual for a dragonfly to reach 30 miles per hour in pursuit of an insect it wants to devour. It can also hover in midair like a miniature helicopter. A dragonfly's favorite hunting grounds are near rivers, streams, and ponds. It likes to eat on the fly, so to speak, enjoying one tasty treat while hunting for its second course.

Dragonflies have compound eyes, with each one made up of as many as 30,000 lenses.

#2

Cheetah

Ahhhh. Too much late-night TV.

When it comes to speed, the cheetah takes the prize for world's fastest land animal. This cat can run up to 70 miles per hour—but only for about the length of two or three football fields, when it begins to overheat. Once it catches and kills its prey, a cheetah has to rest for about half an hour to catch its breath.

The cheetah is built for speed, with its long, greyhound-like frame, lightweight bones, small head, and long legs. The pads on its paws and its sharp claws help it grip the ground for maximum traction, while wide nostrils and large lungs allow it to take the big, deep breaths it needs to power a quick take-off: It can reach 60 miles per hour in only four seconds! The cheetah's long, flat tail acts as a rudder to maintain balance so it can make sharp turns, and its flexible backbone works like a spring, boosting its stride to an incredible 25 feet!

The fovea, an area inside a cheetah's retina, allows the cat to focus with great precision on distant prey. The long, black tear marks under each eye help to lessen the sun's glare.

THAT'S WILD!

SPECIAL REPORT:
Cheetahs in Danger

Not so long ago cheetahs were being killed in great numbers for their beautiful pelts. Although hunting cheetahs is now against the law, these cats are threatened in another way. As the human population increases, the construction of houses and roads limits cheetahs' habitats. In 1900, there were about 100,000 cheetahs in the wild. Today, there are only about 15,000. •

#1 Peregrine Falcon

About the size and weight of a crow, the peregrine falcon is nature's speeding bullet. The fastest animal on Earth, it regularly flies at speeds up to about 55 miles per hour, but when pursuing prey, it can reach almost 70 miles per hour. When performing its spectacular nosedives, it can move even faster.

The peregrine falcon's preferred food is other birds, and when it spots a tasty morsel, it drops into a headfirst dive called a power stoop. As the falcon picks up speed, you can actually hear the roar up to a quarter mile away! Moving as fast as 200 miles per hour, the falcon clenches one foot into a fist-like ball and takes out the prey with a powerful kick. As the bird drops, the falcon swoops underneath to catch it in its talons (claws).

SPECIAL REPORT:
Flying Lessons

Peregrine falcons have taught aerospace engineers a thing or two about high-speed flying. In the past, jet engines would stall out when they reached a certain speed. Scientists who wondered why the same thing didn't happen to peregrine falcons discovered that the birds had a small cone sticking slightly out of each nostril. Just as nature's cones guide air into the falcons' lungs, manmade cones now guide air into jet engines, allowing them to keep operating at extremely high speeds. ●

- In winter, peregrines that breed in northern Canada migrate to South America, a distance of more than 15,000 miles.
- Peregrine falcons usually nest on mountaintops and cliffs, but in cities, they nest on the ledges of tall buildings.

THAT'S WILD!

2 WHAT A STUNT!

Capturing prey can be a real challenge, and some predators have to do some pretty extreme footwork to land their dinner. Fantastic jumps, spectacular leaps, and in some cases, midair acrobatics are all in a day's work for these ten top athletic predators.

#10

Jumping Spider

This small daytime hunter is the bungee-jumping champion of the animal world. Once it spots prey with the two of its eyes that are large and forward-facing, it attaches a silken cord to its jumping-off spot and launches itself toward its unsuspecting victim. If the spider misses, it can simply crawl back up the cord and try again. To jump, the spider produces contractions in its body that force fluids into its back legs, which suddenly straighten out, propelling the spider up to a distance of 2 feet.

#9

Tarsier

The tarsier of Southeast Asia can jump as far as 6 feet and as high as 5 feet, while twisting its body in midair and extending its fingers to grab a branch. Its tail is used for support and balance while its long fingers give it the ability to grasp almost any surface. The tarsier has the largest eyes relative to its overall size than any other animal, and it can swivel its neck 180 degrees in either direction—which helps it spot and catch small prey in pitch darkness.

#7

Flying Snakes

Flying *snakes*? The idea of venomous animals swooping down out of the sky may make you nervous, but don't worry; these tree-dwelling snakes from Asia's rainforests are only mildly venomous. Flying snakes don't really fly either; rather, they jump from tree to tree, flattening their bodies as much as possible and gliding as far as 330 feet through the air.

#8

Serval

The serval has the longest legs for its body size in the cat family and has been known to leap 10 feet up in the air to catch a bird. A medium-size cat, it is found in the savannas of Africa, where it hunts from dusk through dawn. Using its sight and keen hearing to locate prey such as a lizard, rabbit, or even a small antelope, the serval quietly approaches then pounces. Before killing it, however, this cat will often play with its prey.

#6

Mountain Lion

Mountain lions, also called cougars, pumas, or catamounts, are the best jumpers of the cat family, capable of covering 30 feet in a single bound. Their main prey is whitetail deer, but they also feast on elk, rabbit, raccoon, wild pig, armadillo, and birds. Mountain lions are great climbers and can jump to the ground from as high as 60 feet in pursuit of prey. They are most active from dusk through dawn, but have been known to hunt during the daylight hours as well.

#5 Gannet

The gannet is a powerful flier that soars higher than most seabirds. The gannet starts its nosedive from 100 feet in the air. Built-in airbags beneath the skin of its face and chest inflate on impact, allowing the gannet to hit the water at 90 miles per hour without harm. It then continues diving up to 30 feet down, much deeper than most other birds go to chase and capture food. Binocular vision helps this large bird judge distances accurately.

Just five more minutes, Mom.

#4 Sea Otter

Unlike most marine mammals, sea otters do not have a layer of blubber to keep them warm. That's why they are constantly on the move, searching for more food. They will even dive 330 feet to find it. These voracious eaters dine on a wide variety of sea creatures like sea urchins, abalone, mussels, clams, crabs, and snails. It's no wonder that sea otters feel the need to rest after so much activity. They sleep in forests of kelp—long, rubbery plants that grow in the ocean—draping the plants over themselves to act as an anchor so they won't drift away.

Emperor penguins spend several hours a day waterproofing their outer feathers with oil that's produced by a gland below their tail to keep the thick layer of down closest to their skin dry and warm.

THAT'S WILD!

Emperor Penguin

Emperor penguins may not be able to get off the ground, but they sure can fly when they're underwater. The largest of the world's penguins, they perform with an athlete's grace when playing with each other or chasing after cuttlefish, crustaceans (aquatic arthropods with shells and two pairs of antennae), and other small marine animals. Their favorite food items live in the ocean's depths and to find them, emperor penguins will dive as deep as 1,770 feet, deeper than any other bird. They can stay down for up to 20 minutes before surfacing for air.

Penguins use their wings as flippers to push their streamlined bodies through the water. Their tails and webbed feet work like rudders for steering. An emperor penguin's most impressive move is a stunt known as "porpoising." That's when they swim underwater, leap several feet into the air in a long arc, and dive down beneath the surface again.

Last one there is a rotten fish.

Sperm Whale

The sperm whale is the deepest-diving hunter in the sea, reaching depths of up to 7,200 feet—that's more than 1.3 miles! The largest of the toothed whales, the sperm whale can reach 59 feet in length and weigh as much as 45 tons. It also has the biggest head—about 20 feet long, 10 feet high, and 7 feet wide—for its body size of any animal. Perhaps that's why it can dive so deep and resurface without harm.

Sperm whales use echolocation to locate food, making clicking sounds that pulse through the water. Whales "read" the clicks as they bounce back to them, helping them locate prey and determine its size. A sperm whale can consume a ton of food a day. It feeds on skate, octopus, and squid, including the famed giant squid.

Nearly everything we know about this huge deep-sea squid comes from the contents of sperm whale stomachs. Sperm whales and giant squid are pretty evenly matched in size, and the whale comes well equipped for battle with 7-inch-long teeth that weigh 2 pounds apiece. Fights between sperm whales and giant squid are so fierce that sperm whales often resurface with large round wounds made by the squid's toothed suckers.

Whale calves have to breathe more often than adults, so when a mother whale goes on a deep-diving hunt for food, she leaves her calf in the care of other whales that protect it from predators.

Where's my clicker?

THAT'S WILD!

#1 Ruppell's Griffon Vulture

The highest-flying bird in the world, the Ruppell's griffon vulture of central Africa has reached heights of 37,000 feet. How do we know? The pilot of a passenger jet recorded that altitude when a bird flew into the plane in 1973. With a wingspan of about 10 feet, these birds are often seen soaring in pairs, scanning the ground for their favorite kind of meal—dead animals, or better still, a nest full of seabird eggs. Their long necks make it easy for them to reach far into a carcass to strip it of meat. Ruppell's griffon vultures have been known to strip an antelope to the bone within minutes.

Vultures serve a useful purpose. They are like nature's janitors: they clear the land of dead animals before they cause disease. Vultures like to share their meal, so when they spot something tasty, they will fly in circles above an unguarded nest or carcass to let other vultures know that dinner is served. Their bald heads may be unsightly, but they allow the birds to more easily clean themselves, keeping them free of disease-causing germs that form in decaying food.

CHAPTER 3 MASTERS OF DISGUISE

For many predators, the best way to get a meal is to keep a low profile, and blending in with their environment helps them do it. Camouflage and mimicry are the perfect weapons for predators that are planning a sneak attack—and here are ten of the most extreme masters of disguise.

#9 Cuttlefish

The cuttlefish belongs to the same group of animals as octopus and squid. A true master of disguise, the cuttlefish can change color and even texture to blend in almost perfectly with its surroundings. Its skin is covered with special cells that reflect light in many different colors. When an unsuspecting sea creature swims by, the innocent-looking rock or hunk of coral comes to life—and pops the animal into its mouth for dinner.

#10 Snow Leopard

Snow leopards are found at high elevations in the mountains of central Asia, where they hunt for a large variety of prey including yaks, goats, sheep, boars, and ibex. Their prey never sees them coming—until it's too late. In the mountain ranges where snow leopards hunt, there are no trees to hide behind, just rocks. Their white, yellowish, or smoky gray fur is dotted with darker rosette-shaped spots, making them almost invisible in their rocky hunting ground.

#8

Angel Shark

The angel shark spends the daylight hours buried in the sand on the sea floor, perfectly camouflaged by its gray, brown, and black coloring. It lies there in ambush, waiting for small fish to swim within gulping distance. When an unsuspecting fish comes near, the shark lunges upward, throws open its gigantic mouth, sucks the fish in, and swallows it whole. When darkness falls, it emerges from its hiding spot and forages more actively.

#7

Carnivorous Caterpillar

Scientists used to believe that all caterpillars were harmless vegetarians. Not so! It turns out that there are a few meat-eating caterpillars. In Hawaii, for example, there live several members of the Eupithecia moth family. While members of this moth family are found all over the world, only the Hawaiian species have become killers. Their color, shape, and posture help them blend invisibly into tree branches. Small hairs and nerves on their backs clue them in when an insect comes near. In a fraction of a second, the caterpillar can snap backward and grab its meal with pincer-tipped forelegs.

#6

Orchid Mantis

Beware the beautiful orchids that bloom in the Malaysian rainforest—they hide a beast. Perched on its petals, exactly matching the color and texture of the orchid flower, is the orchid mantis. It waits motionless for its next meal to walk by: insects looking to snack on the orchid's nectar. When a potential victim approaches, the mantis attacks with lightning speed, impaling the prey on its leg spikes.

#5 Firefly

Male fireflies, you are on alert! There's a female firefly out there that's got your number. Females of the *Photuris* firefly group have discovered how to mimic the flashing code of another group. They send out a glowing invitation to males of the *Photinus* group that might be passing, but when a male answers such a call, he doesn't get a mate—he gets eaten.

#4 Death Adder

Unlike many snakes, the common death adder of Australia doesn't actively search for prey. Instead, this snake sits in one place and waits for prey to come to it. First, it covers its coiled-up body with leaves. Once its disguise is in place, it wiggles the tip of its tail to lure prey. When an animal like a frog, lizard, or even a bird approaches to investigate the movement, the death adder quickly strikes, injecting its lethal venom! Today, death adder bites rarely cause human fatalities because they can be treated with antivenin. In the past, however, the bites used to result in death more than 50 percent of the time.

#3 Snapping Turtle

This turtle eats just about anything, but when given a choice, it chooses fish for dinner. Snapping turtles are expert fishermen. They hang out at the muddy bottoms of deep rivers, lakes, and ponds, staying below for about 50 minutes at a time. A dusty brown-colored shell covers its body, making it hard for prey to tell which part of its environment is mud and which part is turtle. Its mottled skin and the algae that grow on its shell make the turtle even harder to find. When an unsuspecting victim swims by, the turtle opens its mouth to reveal the perfect lure: a wiggly, worm-like tongue. Then—snap!—goes the turtle and down goes the fish.

What's the rush?

#2 Leafy Sea Dragon

Found in temperate waters around Australia, the leafy sea dragon sports attachments that look exactly like seaweed. This relative of the seahorse uses its nearly invisible fins, one at the base of its neck and another near its tail, to propel it through the water. As it moves slowly along, swaying back and forth with the currents, the leafy sea dragon is completely hidden by its brilliant disguise. Prey doesn't even recognize it as a fish and neither do predators. Undisturbed, the sea dragon floats serenely along, sucking up the tiny shrimp it eats.

SPECIAL REPORT:
Flying Lessons

Leafy sea dragons are quite beautiful and are often captured for sale to collectors who keep them in private aquariums. Today, leafy sea dragons are considered an endangered species, and the Australian government has passed laws making it illegal for anyone to hunt or sell them. •

#1 Deep-sea Anglerfish

In the depths of the sea where no sunlight filters down, many species have developed very unique coping skills. Take the female anglerfish, for example. Attached to this creature is a modified fin that looks like a fishing rod with a glowing lure at its end. This glow attracts prey like moths to a light bulb—and that's exactly the idea. As fish swim toward it, the anglerfish waits with gaping jaws—and in a flash, gulps down its fish dinner.

What makes the anglerfish's lure light up? A small organ at the tip is filled with millions of bacteria that produce light. This process of producing light (in other words, light created by living animals) is called bioluminescence. An anglerfish uses its lure to fish for its food, just the way a human fishes. And prey find it irresistible!

Some types of male anglerfish have only one purpose in life: to find a female and fasten himself to her body. For the rest of his life he remains there, fertilizing the female's eggs while she provides him with nutrients.

THAT'S WILD!

Rah, rah, sis boom ba. Go, team. Go!

4 SUPER SENSES

Just imagine what it would be like to be able to smell a fish in the water a mile away. How amazing would it be to hear a sound in another town or find your way out of a forest without using your eyes? Some animals do that each and every day—and the following ten predators have developed some truly extreme senses.

#9

Sand Scorpion

The sand scorpion is blind, but that doesn't keep it from a mouthful of moth when it's hungry. This arthropod lacks sight, hearing, and smell, but is far from helpless. It relies on two kinds of extremely sensitive touch receptors. One type responds to sound waves made at the ground's surface, and the other notes vibrations in the sand. If you drop just a single grain of sand near a sand scorpion, it will move toward it in a flash!

#10

Eagle

Eagles hunt their prey during the day with eyes that outperform the highest-powered binoculars. They are also equipped with wickedly sharp, hooked beaks and large clawed feet to help them make the kill. Eagles are found all over the world except in arctic regions. Large and powerful, they prey on animals such as sloths, monkeys, pigs, and fish.

Bald eagles aren't really bald. Instead, they get their name from an old English word that means "white."

THAT'S WILD!

#8

Star-nosed Mole

The wiggly pink projections at the end of this mole's nose may look weird to humans, but they give this animal what might be called the best sense of touch on the planet. The 22 "fingers" on the mole's nose have an incredible 100,000 nerve fibers running through them. As the mole digs for prey, those "fingers" are always at work touching and identifying things. As a result, the star-nosed mole can identify and eat a tasty tidbit like a grub or worm faster than a person can think!

#7

Wolf

Given the right atmospheric conditions, the wolf can use its sense of smell to locate prey from up to 1.5 miles away. In fact, it can detect a scent 100,000 times better than a human can. The wolf's hearing is quite amazing, too. Depending on the environment, the wolf can hear an animal's cry from 6 to 10 miles away! Between these two weapons, a wolf can track down large prey, such as deer, moose, elk, and caribou, as well as smaller animals, like beavers, rabbits, squirrels, and mice.

I gotta cut back on the snacks.

#6

Owl

Owls have such sensitive hearing that they can hear the sounds of small rodents as they move through the leaves and find them with pinpoint accuracy. They have special adaptations that help them do this. Many owl species have asymmetrical ears—in other words, one ear is lower than the other. This gives them binocular hearing, like people have binocular vision. In addition, owls have feathers on their face that help guide sounds to the ears. You can see this really well on barn owls, which can catch prey in complete darkness, all because of their incredible hearing.

#5

Bat

The only mammal capable of flight, the bat uses echolocation both to navigate and to find food in the dark. How does echolocation work? While flying, the bat sends out calls so high-pitched that human beings can't hear them. The sound waves made as these calls bounce off objects in the bat's environment give the bat clues as to the object's location. A bat's sonar is so precise it can distinguish between objects separated by as little as twice the width of a human hair!

Hey buddy, off my tail!

#4

Black Dragonfish

While most bioluminescent creatures make blue light, which travels farther and is visible to all creatures, the black dragonfish emits red light. Only a few fish can see red light, and they all belong to the dragonfish family. Nearly every part of this fish's body lights up, including its belly and organs under its eyes. Thanks to its red light, this deep-sea fish can hunt in complete darkness. Since only other dragonfish can see its light, this sneaky fish uses it as a laser beam to hone in on prey without giving away its own presence.

#3

Pit Viper

Some of the deadliest creatures on Earth, pit vipers include such snakes as water moccasins and rattlesnakes. They are equipped with needle-like fangs filled with lethal venom. Worse, it's almost impossible to hide from them. That's because the pit-shaped organs between the eye and the nostril on a pit viper's head are sensitive to infrared radiation. Like heat-seeking missiles, these snakes can detect changes in temperature of only fractions of a degree. This feature allows pit vipers to detect the presence of animals with body temperatures only slightly different from the surrounding environment. Once prey is located, these fierce predators can strike with deadly precision even in total darkness.

#2

Mantis Shrimp

The mantis shrimp gets its name from the fact that it looks and hunts a lot like the praying mantis insect. But that's where the similarity ends. This shrimp is so powerful that it has been known to use its club-like claws to smash aquarium glass. A fearsome carnivore, it will eat just about anything that doesn't eat it first—and with its amazing vision, it has no trouble locating its prey!

The mantis shrimp not only has color receptors for ultraviolet and infrared light that let it see a much broader array of colors than any other creature, but also three separate "pupils" at the end of each eye stalk. This gives it trinocular vision in each eye. (Humans have binocular vision but require two eyes for it to work.) Scientists think this allows the mantis shrimp to see prey that appears invisible to creatures with lesser powers of sight.

#1 Hammerhead Shark

The hammerhead shark wins the number one spot in the super sense category. Like many sharks, the hammerhead has amazing senses of smell and touch. But the hammerhead, with its bizarrely shaped head, has more room for the most advanced sensory equipment. Its eyes are set so far apart that it can't see something straight in front of it, yet that ends up working in the shark's favor. As the fish swings its head back and forth, it gets a panoramic view of its surroundings.

This shark's broad head also stores more electroreceptors than other sharks, which makes it tops at hunting out buried food treasure like flounder and rays. Think of a metal detector and you'll get the idea! But by far its most extraordinary feature is that it may have its own built-in global positioning system. Some scientists think that hammerhead sharks can navigate by using their electroreception to detect Earth's magnetic fields!

Great hammerhead sharks can reach a length of 20 feet and weigh over 1,000 pounds.

Anyone got some nails?

THAT'S WILD!

5 STEALTH WARFARE

Some of the most successful animal predators can be downright sneaky. Their favorite hunting method is to wait for prey to come to them. Others devise ways to trap their unsuspecting victims. Either way, the prey never knows what hit it! Here are ten of the most extremely sneaky predators in the animal kingdom.

#9

Red Fox

They don't call the red fox sly for nothing! A fox's usual manner of hunting is to ambush its prey. When hunger strikes, it stands motionless under the cover of foliage or high grass, listening and watching with great concentration. When a small animal, like a rabbit, wanders close enough, the fox leaps high into the air and lands on its prey, pinning the victim with its front paws. Sometimes this clever hunter plays dead to fool birds that might try to share in the kill, and then it ambushes them as well.

#10

Ambush Bug

The ambush bug certainly lives up to its name. It finds a nice spot on a flower head and remains as still as can be while it waits for some tasty nectar- or pollen-eater to crawl by. Then, in a flash, it attacks. Grabbing its victim with strong, mantid-like legs, the ambush bug stabs it with its beak and injects the prey with fluids strong enough to dissolve its insides. Then the ambush bug slurps up its liquid lunch.

#8

Sand Diver Lizardfish

The sand diver lizardfish is found in the waters around North Carolina all the way south into the Gulf of Mexico. With its cigar-like body, it easily burrows beneath the sand or it simply waits motionless, completely hidden by its sandy coloration. This sneaky fish waits until a tasty morsel floats by, then up it pops to grab its meal before the prey has a chance to swim away.

#7

Ant Lion

The ant lion isn't an ant or a lion but the larval stage of an insect that got its name because it's a wily hunter of ants and other insects. Ant lions that live in sandy areas catch their meals in circular pits lined with sand that are usually about 2 inches wide and 2 inches deep. Whatever falls in ends up in the savage jaws of these clever little predators waiting below, buried in the sand. The larva sticks out its head, opens its jaws, and lunch is served!

#6

Gladiator Spider

Also called the ogre-faced spider, this night-hunting arachnid has an unusual way of ambushing prey. Holding a small, stretchy web with its four front legs, the gladiator spider hangs upside down a few inches above the ground, waiting for an insect to pass beneath. As soon as its prey is within range, the spider drops the net—and captures a tasty midnight treat.

Ha ha, I can still see you!

Trapdoor Spider

This spider uses camouflage, but it's to hide a trap instead of its body. Trapdoor spiders dig burrows in the ground, complete with hinged lids made of bits of plants and soil. At night the spider holds the door nearly closed with its mouthparts. It has special sensory hairs on its legs that can detect vibrations in the ground. When prey passes by, the spider lunges from its hiding place and strikes. Then it drags its victim into the burrow below.

#4

Great Horned Owl

The great horned owl is equipped with the best kind of feathers to make a stealth attack—they are totally silent! Prey can't hear the whir of its wings as it swoops down because this owl's outer, primary feathers have a jagged, "saw-tooth" edge. The jagged edge breaks up the air as it passes over the wing so that there's no noise at all. The soft, round-edged secondary feathers also reduce noise, contributing to the great horned owl's ability to move through the air without making a sound.

Comin' at ya!

I told those two to hide, not just stand there!

#3

Lion

When it comes to hunting, female lions are among the sneakiest predators on the planet. As four hunting females approach a herd of hoofed animals, two find hiding places. The other two roam around the outskirts of the herd to a spot opposite their hidden counterparts. Then they start to close in. When the prey spies the two herding lions bounding toward them, they panic and run the other way—right into the jaws of the two lions that are hiding! The strategy they use is the lion equivalent of "divide and conquer."

- An adult humpback whale's heart weighs about 450 pounds—the equivalent of three average-sized humans!
- Male humpback whales are known for their long, beautiful songs made up of repeating patterns of groans, roaring sounds, chirps, and trills. As the whales sing mostly during the breeding season, the songs are probably related to mating, but scientists are not sure exactly how.

THAT'S WILD!

#2

Humpback Whale

Humpback whales are highly social animals that stay together in groups called pods. They get their name from their unique habit of arching their backs as they leap from the water in preparation for their next dive. These whales also have a unique method of fishing called bubble-net feeding. Up to 30 whales dive deep beneath a school of herring or other fish and swim in a circle around them. The whales blow out their breath as they swim, creating a "net" of bubbles. Then as some of the humpbacks continue blowing bubbles to keep the fish "corralled" in the bubble net, others dive deeper, making extremely loud vocal sounds to scare and confuse the herring. The fish try to get away by swimming up to the surface, where they are ambushed by the rest of the pod. With their mouths wide open, the whales can make quick work of the herring.

#1 Amazonian Ant

A type of tiny ant in the Amazon rainforest has developed a gruesome way to capture prey much bigger than itself. Worker ants cut fine hair-like fibers from the plant on which they live. They weave the fibers together into a framework. Topping it with a specially cultivated fungus that dries into a substance like fiberglass, the ants then puncture holes in the spongy mass, just big enough to poke their heads through. Lurking in the holes, these extremely skillful predators grab the legs and antennae of any unsuspecting insect that lands on the framework. Then they pin their prey to the mat, stretching them out and holding them as their nest mates swarm in for the kill. Once the prey is subdued, it's cut up into bite-sized bits and fed to the young.

I said keep your head down!

CHAPTER 6 GANG WARFARE

For many predators, cooperative hunting is a win-win situation. By hunting with other members of their species, they can take down much larger prey than they could take down alone. That means more than enough food for everybody, and the predators don't have to hunt as often. Here are ten of the most extremely cooperative hunters.

#10

Jackal

Found throughout Africa and Asia, jackals have coloration that helps them hunt under cover. Their fur is gold, black, silver, or striped, depending on the colors found at their hunting grounds. The only member of the dog family to mate for life, jackals live in close-knit groups. Once prey is spotted, the whole group works together to bring it down. These noisy creatures communicate with each other using a wide array of yips, howls, barks, and yelps. Each family member recognizes and understands its own group's patterns of "speech."

#9

Wolf

Wolves are noted for their ability to overpower really big animals such as elk, bison, and antelope. They manage it by hunting in groups called packs. Each member of the wolf pack has a role depending on its rank. There are usually two leaders called alpha wolves, a male and a female. The lead wolves let the others know that a hunt is on by howling. Wolves on a hunt travel single file, with one of the alpha wolves leading the way. They succeed in making a kill only about once in 13 tries. It's no wonder that when they do succeed, wolves will gobble up 20 pounds of meat at a time!

#8 Dolphin

By banding together in large groups called pods, dolphins have figured out the best way to catch the fast-moving schools of fish they like to eat. Using echolocation, the pod spreads out in the water like one giant sea creature. Scanning the water with sound waves as a group, the pod can cover much more territory than one dolphin ever could alone.

Some dolphins have learned to cooperate with humans during runs of fish like mullet. They signal to let the fishers know when to cast their nets. In return, the humans give the dolphins part of their catch.

THAT'S WILD!

#7 White Pelican

White pelicans live together in large groups called colonies. At dinnertime, these social creatures even feed cooperatively, which is rare behavior in birds. In a horseshoe formation, the pelicans surround schools of fish in shallow water. Then, scooping them up in their pouches, they have one large, sloppy dinner party. Pelicans take in both water and fish, and then hold their bills up vertically to drain out the water before swallowing the food.

#6 Bluefish

Did you know that bluefish will eat just about anything they can catch? They will even kill animals they don't need to eat! Bluefish—a common food fish in the United States—have a mouthful of viciously sharp teeth, just like piranhas do. They average a little over a foot long and travel in large groups, or schools, of other individuals that are all about the same size. When they get riled up in a feeding frenzy, they have been known to attack almost anything that gets in their way.

African Wild Dog

African wild dogs live in packs of 6 to 20 individuals. Like football players before an important game, the dogs have their own special ritual to pump themselves up for a hunt. They circle among themselves, whining, barking, and touching each member of the pack before setting out. When prey is spotted, the dogs run the animal to exhaustion. The wild dogs don't get tired themselves because they take turns being the leader. Some of the dogs run close to the animal, while others follow behind at a slower pace. As the leaders tire, they switch positions.

Nile Crocodile

Some observers have reported seeing large groups of Nile crocodiles working together to capture and kill large animals. They have a unique way of biting off a chunk of meat by clamping down and then spinning until a section of the carcass comes free. This technique works even better when there are other crocodiles around to provide an anchor. Nile crocodiles will also gang up on a school of fish and herd them into the shallows for everyone to share.

Sometimes large prey carcasses have been found underwater, held down by branches. Scientists think this is an example of primitive tool use: A lone crocodile bracing the carcass on a branch to tear off more meat.

THAT'S WILD!

Chimpanzee

Until recently scientists thought that chimpanzees ate nothing but fruit, leaves, and an occasional termite snack. All that changed after Jane Goodall, the foremost authority on chimpanzee behavior, saw a chimpanzee share a meal of bush pig with another chimp. Not long afterward, she got the chance to observe a group of chimps go on a hunt. She watched as the group worked together to attack and kill prey. This time, the prey was a colobus monkey. One of the chimps chased it up a tree. Several others blocked the monkey's escape routes, while one of the young male chimps quietly crept up, captured, and killed it. It is now known that chimps regularly hunt prey in small groups. Hunts often take place in times of drought when plant food is scarce.

SPECIAL REPORT:
Losing Ground

Chimpanzee habitat continues to be lost for lumber, to build roads, and to clear land for farming. Before 1960, there were over one million chimpanzees living in more than 25 African countries. Today only six African countries are home to wild chimps, of which only about 200,000 remain. •

#2

Orca

Orcas, also called killer whales, hunt in pods, herding fish into a small area so they can surround and capture them with ease. Orcas have even been observed herding other whales—chasing, biting, and wearing them down until they're too exhausted to fight back. Orcas will spy-hop (poke their heads out of water) or make flying leaps to locate seals, penguins, and other animals resting on ice floes. When they spot a few, they'll create a wave to wash over the floe, knocking the prey into the water. Waiting below are other orcas in the pod, ready to make the kill. In one instance, the pod of orcas was observed returning the prey to the ice floe so the younger orcas in the pod could practice the very same technique!

#1 Driver Ant

Native to Africa, driver ants live in colonies of more than 20 million individuals. Although completely blind, they are still able to communicate with each other through scents called pheromones. Once the call goes out to attack, nothing can stop the ant tide. No other insect has a greater impact on its local environment. They move into a village in a crawling swarm more than 15 yards wide. These ants are not equipped with stingers, but they don't need them. They swarm into the mouths, noses, and ears of anything that gets in their way, killing them by suffocation. Caged or penned animals are defenseless against a swarm of these killers.

In communities plagued by mice or roaches, driver ants, which make excellent exterminators, are considered beneficial.

THAT'S WILD!

7 CHEMICAL WARFARE

Venomous animals use toxins or poisons to kill prey, to defend themselves from other predators, or both. Their deadly brews may be delivered through tentacles, fangs, stingers, or a proboscis. Prepare to meet ten of the most venomous animals (at least to their prey) on Earth.

#10

Shrew

With its sharp teeth, long claws, and poisonous saliva, the shrew packs a mighty punch, especially for such a small animal. This mammal has an extremely fast metabolism, so it must consume its body weight in slugs, worms, snails, and insects every day of the year. Some shrew species use echolocation to find their prey, emitting high-pitched squeals that bounce back to them. This fierce little predator is one of just four species of mammals that are venomous.

#9

Gila Monster

Found mainly in North American deserts, the Gila monster is a slow-moving lizard about 2 feet long that dines on animals such as snakes, birds, frogs, rats, and smaller lizards. This lizard finds food with sensors located on its long tongue—it actually tastes for scent particles left by prey—then it pounces, biting down on its victim. The Gila monster's venom flows down its grooved teeth into the wound, so the longer it chews, the more venom is delivered.

#8

Stingray

This normally passive animal packs a powerful defense mechanism. When threatened, the stingray instantly flicks its long tail at its would-be attacker. As the tail makes contact, the barbed spine inside breaks through the ray's skin and rips into its victim, delivering powerful venom at the same time. The backward-facing barbs make it difficult to remove the sting and worsen the wound. Waders are sometimes attacked when they accidentally step on a stingray hidden in the sand. Attacks are painful and dangerous, but if treated quickly, are seldom fatal.

#7

Sydney Funnel-web Spider

This Australian spider is often called the most venomous spider in the world. Males are more dangerous than females, because they go wandering in search of mates, sometimes ending up in people's houses or garages, while females rarely leave their burrows. Male Sydney funnel-web spiders also have more potent venom than females. Fortunately, since the introduction of an antivenin, no human deaths have been recorded.

The venom of Sydney funnel-web spiders is more toxic to humans than to other mammals, such as dogs and cats.

THAT'S WILD!

#6

Yellow Fat-tailed Scorpion

The yellow fat-tailed scorpion is found in Africa and Asia, and its scientific name, *Androctonus australis*, means "southern man killer." More people die from this scorpion's sting than from any other species. Another very lethal variety is the Brazilian yellow scorpion. They like to hide out in termite nests, but now that so much of their habitat has been destroyed, they are finding their way into cities. With medical care, a sting from most species of scorpion is seldom fatal.

#5

Stonefish

If you step on a stonefish, 13 is definitely an unlucky number! Thirteen is the number of venom-filled spines on the back of this bottom dweller, and that venom is what keeps the stonefish, which is found in shallow, tropical areas of the Indian and Pacific Oceans, fairly safe from predators. Its mottled color is difficult to see in coral reefs and it sometimes uses its pectoral fins to bury itself in the sand along the water's edge. A sting from a stonefish causes terrible pain and a great deal of swelling. Stings can also result in muscle weakness, temporary paralysis, and shock, and symptoms are more severe depending on how many spines have punctured the skin.

> Well, my mom says I'm cute.

#4

Blue-ringed Octopus

The size of a golf ball, the blue-ringed octopus inhabits reefs and tidepools, ranging from Australia to Japan. This predator is equipped with two kinds of venom—one to kill prey, and another to subdue anything that gets in its way. Small, beautiful, and deadly, the blue-ringed octopus delivers venom 10,000 times more potent than cyanide. Within minutes of being bitten, paralysis sets in. Unless treatment is started immediately, the victim may well die.

- If you can see the blue rings on this octopus, you are too close! When calm, this animal is brown. The blue rings only appear when it is excited enough to strike.
- The blue-ringed octopus doesn't make its own venom—it gets help from toxin-producing bacteria that live in its salivary glands.

THAT'S WILD!

Cone Shell

Cone shells are marine snails, and like most snails, they are not speedy. However, they are far from defenseless. Found throughout the world, these reef-dwellers hide a deadly weapon within their shells. If they sense prey, they extend a long tube called a proboscis equipped with a modified "tongue" (radula) that acts like a harpoon. The cone shell shoots the harpoon, which injects a fast-acting poison that paralyzes its victim, then it reels it back to eat. Three species, including the tulip cone shell, have venom strong enough to kill humans. The only treatment for a cone shell sting is to keep the patient alive through artificial respiration until the venom's effects wear off.

Scientists have recently discovered that some of the toxins in cone shell venom may work as painkillers. They would like to do more research, but these animals are fast disappearing because collectors favor their beautiful shells.

THAT'S WILD!

Inland Taipan Snake

You don't want to tangle with the inland Taipan snake! This Australian native is considered the most poisonous snake on Earth: One bite contains a complex brew of more than 50 toxins, enough to kill 100 people. The inland Taipan's venom can cause death in two different ways. First, it scrambles the neurons in the brain that control muscles, causing paralysis. As the poison spreads, the victim can suffer a range of symptoms from severe headaches and nausea to convulsions and coma. Second, it prevents blood from clotting, causing uncontrollable bleeding. Taipan venom works quickly, so the snake can take out fast-moving prey such as rats without getting hurt in the process.

#2

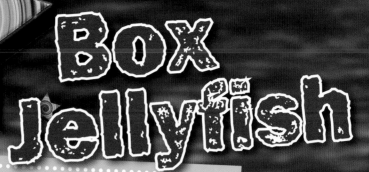

#1 Box Jellyfish

Box jellyfish are transparent so you can barely see them in the water. They've got no bones or brains, but these jellies just might be the most dangerous creatures in the sea. With enough venom to kill up to 60 humans in just one of its stinging cells, these lethal creatures have killed more people in Australia than stonefish, sharks, and crocodiles combined.

Unlike most jellies that drift where the currents take them, box jellyfish can propel themselves through the water. They get their name from the distinctly four-cornered shape of their bodies, or bells. Up to 15 tentacles grow from each corner of the bell and each tentacle has about 5,000 stinging cells! Scientists believe this jellyfish developed its powerful venom to instantly paralyze prey and avoid breakage of its delicate tentacles. Death from paralysis can occur from within 30 seconds to 15 minutes. Even a mild sting is very painful and leaves long-lasting scars. But don't worry. Careful watch is kept in swimming areas where these jellyfish are found, so beach-goers are warned to stay out of the water when they show up.

With its tentacles stretched out, the box jellyfish can measure 6 feet in length. The bell is about the size of a basketball.

THAT'S WILD!

CHAPTER 8 REALLY WEIRD

Certain predators are like no others. With extremely odd-looking body parts and bizarre behaviors to match, many of these creatures look as if they are a science experiment gone wrong. The truth is that the following ten predators are equipped with exactly what they need to do their job—which is to find and kill the kind of prey they need to survive.

#10

Honeypot Ant

With stomachs that grow as big as small grapes, honeypot ants called repletes hang upside down in clusters and gorge on the food the worker ants bring them. Though honeypot ants hunt for termites and other small insects as well as collect pollen and honeydew, they live in dry areas of western North America, where food is sometimes limited. So when food is scarce, the repletes repay the colony by regurgitating "honey" to feed the other ants.

#9

Chameleon

The toes on each of this lizard's feet have fused into two opposing digits, so the chameleon can easily hang onto branches. It can use its tail to help hold on or stretch it out for balance. The chameleon's ability to change color according to its mood also helps conceal it from unsuspecting prey, while its eyes can move around independently of each other. When it spots a tasty meal, the chameleon zaps out its long tongue, captures the bug with the sticky end, and yanks it back to eat.

Gotcha!

48

Egg-eating Snake

These amazing snakes from Africa and India eat nothing but eggs. An extra bone in an egg-eating snake's jaw allows it to open its mouth super wide, enough to swallow eggs more than twice the diameter of its body. After the snake swallows the egg, tooth-like structures in the back of the snake's throat break it. The egg's contents are digested while the broken shell comes up again the same way it went down. Burp!

I'll take mine over-easy, please.

#6

Giant Anteater

Able to stick its tongue out almost 2 feet, the giant anteater has the longest tongue in the world. It uses its sharp claws to break into ant nests, then uses its sticky tongue to lap up the ants. This creature has been known to eat about 30,000 ants in just one day, but it doesn't eat them all from only one nest. Instead, it leaves enough ants in each nest it visits for the colony to rebuild, thus securing its food supply.

#7

Matamata

With its flattened head, snorkel-like snout, and long, fringed neck, the matamata is one weird-looking turtle. Resting motionless on the bottom of shallow, slow-moving water, the matamata easily blends into the background. Some experts suggest its neck fringes not only provide camouflage but also help the turtle detect prey. When a fish swims by, the matamata opens its gaping mouth and expands its neck, sucking in fish and water like a vacuum cleaner. It then closes its mouth, slowly expels the water, and swallows the fish whole.

#5

Tarantula

These large hairy spiders live in warm regions all around the world. Most tarantulas have weak venom, and their bites are no more serious than a bee sting. But tarantulas that live in the Americas have another way to defend themselves. They have a layer of barbed hairs (called urticating hairs) covering their abdomen. When threatened, they quickly kick these hairs off, launching them at their target. The hairs cause irritation, especially to the eyes and nose, and if inhaled by a small animal, can cause severe enough swelling to result in suffocation.

The itching powder that was once sold in novelty stores was made from the urticating hairs of tarantulas.

THAT'S WILD!

#4

Archerfish

The archerfish can shoot insects out of the air with the accuracy of a rifle. What makes this feat particularly unusual is that the archerfish has to be able to see accurately through water as well as through air in order to aim, even though water distorts images. Further, archerfish can't do this by instinct; they have to learn how. The fish shoots by pressing its tongue against a groove on the roof of its mouth. Then it snaps its gills shut to launch a jet of water at a tempting morsel.

Dragonfly Nymph

The aquatic dragonfly nymph—the young, wingless stage of a dragonfly—has an unusual of way hunting. When this voracious predator spots prey, it uses a deadly harpoon to spear lunch—its own lower lip, usually kept folded under its head! The dragonfly nymph has deadly accuracy thanks to its vision. Unlike most insects (but just like humans), the nymph's two big eyes have an area where the vision overlaps. This means it can clearly focus on its target and accurately judge the best place to strike. The lower lip hits in less than 25 milliseconds, and hooks the prey so it can't escape.

#2 Carnivorous Snails

Like other snails, carnivorous snails don't have jaws to chew their food. Instead, they have a handy little "tongue" called a radula. Unlike the radula of their plant-eating relatives, however, the radula of carnivorous snails is covered with up to 750,000 tiny backward-facing dagger-shaped spines. These spines make it not only easy to capture prey, but also to hold onto it. The rosy wolf snail tracks smaller snails by following their slime. Another type of carnivorous snail produces an acid in a gland in its foot. When its favorite prey, the round-mouthed snail, withdraws into its shell and closes the opening, the carnivorous snail simply uses the acid to dissolve its prey's shell.

Carnivorous snails are found in water as well as land. Some of these sea snails use their radula to drill a hole through the shells of their prey in order to get at the tasty contents inside. Whelks, however, jam their big foot between the shells of blue mussels to prevent them from closing before using the radula to pull them out. Thanks to radula, some of the world's slowest animals have become extremely efficient predators.

#1 Platypus

The platypus has to be considered a wonder of the natural world. Sporting the bill and webbed feet of a duck, the tail of a beaver, and the fur and claws of an otter, this mammal—which is hatched from an egg—appears to be an animal designed by committee. This weird collection of physical traits, however, actually turns out to be an extremely successful predator.

An excellent swimmer, the platypus uses its webbed feet as paddles and its tail as a rudder to steer it through freshwater lakes and rivers. Its sensitive bill helps it hunt down prey that's buried in the mud. After the platypus detects worms, insects, or shellfish, it scoops them up, along with a mouthful of gravel and mud. Storing the gravel and grit in its cheek pouches, it resurfaces to eat. The gravel helps the otherwise toothless platypus to grind up the food so it can be digested. Once on land, its webbed feet reveal a set of claws that help the platypus dig a burrow to make a home in.

The male platypus has a sharp, hollow spur filled with venom above each back heel for self-defense.

THAT'S WILD!

9 CRUNCH!

Predators with extremely powerful jaws and teeth have a definite advantage when dealing with prey. Their bone-crunching ability not only aids them in subduing their prey, but also in devouring and digesting it. Here are the ten animals you'd least like to get bitten by.

Left, right, left, right, left!

#10

Wide-mouth Frog

Found in the ponds of Argentina, the wide-mouth frog is known for its tremendous appetite. It has an extra set of tiny cone-shaped teeth on the roof of its mouth that are not for chewing but for clamping down on prey. Extremely aggressive, this predator will chomp down on anything that moves and won't let go—even if it means choking to death!

#9

Army Ant

The army ants of South America live in groups of up to a million. And when they go on the march, army ants will eat as many as 100,000 bugs a day. The blind worker ants are protected by soldier ants, which have large heads and sickle-shaped jaws (mandibles) that are so strong they can cut through leather. However, the soldier ants' jaws are so big they can only eat if the workers feed them.

It's said that Native Americans once used army ants as sutures. They'd hold the ants near the wound and pinch them so their jaws would shut and hold the edges of the wound together. The ant's body was then removed, leaving the jaws in place until the wound healed.

THAT'S WILD!

Wind Scorpion

Pound for pound this hairy, nocturnal arachnid has a much deadlier set of jaws (chelicerae) than a great white shark. In fact, this creature has the strongest jaws—relative to size—of any animal on Earth. A wind scorpion's jaws make short work of its victims and have been known to snap a grasshopper in two with one bite.

#7

Snapping Turtle

Unlike most turtles, snapping turtles are not well protected by their shells. Their bottom shells are so small, they can't pull themselves in to hide. Perhaps that's why they're so fierce. On land, they raise up their bodies and with jaws open and ready to snap, they lunge at intruders. Though they have no teeth, snapping turtles use their sharp beaks and powerful jaws to grind up the fish, frogs, and snakes they like to eat. These fearless reptiles have even been known to attack people.

#6

Tasmanian Devil

Australia's Tasmanian devil has a bite as strong as a dog three times its weight. This extremely ferocious marsupial scares off predators with its ear-splitting scream. It hunts at night for prey such as wallabies and wombats, then completely devours them—bones and all

Give me back my dolly.

55

#5

Leopard Seal

Using its strong jaws and long, razor-sharp teeth, the leopard seal rips apart the flesh of prey such as southern fur seals and penguins, two of its favorite meals. One of the Antarctic's fiercest creatures, the leopard seal will kill a penguin quickly then use its teeth to skin it, shaking it free of its feathery covering. Weighing in at 1,000 pounds and reaching a length of 12 feet, the leopard seal is one predator to avoid at all costs!

The leopard seal is one of the few marine mammals that preys on other marine mammals.

THAT'S WILD!

Wow! Who's your dentist?

#4

Jaguar

Of all the big cats, jaguars, which are found in the rainforests of Central and South America, have the most powerful jaws and teeth. Unlike other big cats, jaguars kill with a single bite to the skull rather than the neck, a tactic that comes in handy when taking a mouthful of turtle. Jaguars are the only animals capable of biting through their rock-hard shells! Jaguars also eat many other kinds of prey, including monkeys, anteaters, deer, and cattle.

#3

Hyena

Hyenas are the owners of some of the most powerful jaws in the animal kingdom. These animals also come fitted out with a set of sharp teeth that are just the thing for cracking the bones of their prey so they can get to the soft marrow inside. Hyenas are such voracious eaters that one hyena can consume up to a third of its body weight in one feeding frenzy. These animals do not waste any part of their kill, eating not only the flesh, but also the hide, hair, skin, teeth, hooves, and bones of their prey. Bones make up such a large part of their diet that hyena droppings are almost always white.

So, what did you order?

#2

Crocodile

Crocodiles are the closest things to living dinosaurs. Their design is so perfect that they've hardly changed at all in the last 100 million years. A large crocodile is strong enough to pull a full-grown wildebeest completely off its feet. Crocodiles have as many as 68 teeth that can grow as long as 3 inches. They use their teeth to grab and pierce their prey. To pull it apart, all the croc has to do is tear along the dotted line—of puncture marks! A fully-grown crocodile can bear down on prey with up to a ton and half of pressure. Crocodiles possess the strongest stomach juices of any vertebrate, which helps them digest even the thickest piece of bone or horn. Because they're so good at conserving energy, large crocodiles can go without food for up to a year, living off fats stored in their tails. Today, crocodiles can be found in the warm regions of more than 90 countries.

A crocodile can leap as high as 10 feet straight up out of the water to snatch a bird right out of the air!

THAT'S WILD!

58

Great White Shark

The great white shark weighs as much as 2,000 pounds, but its skeleton consists mostly of cartilage rather than bone, making this killing machine extremely buoyant. Its torpedo shape is tailor-made for quick pursuit. Its roughly 3,000 teeth are arranged in multiple rows in its mouth. Should a shark lose one of its pearly whites, a new tooth moves forward conveyor belt–style to replace it. Each replacement tooth is slightly larger than the one that came before it—to keep pace with the shark as it grows. A single great white shark can run through more than 50,000 teeth in a lifetime. And what amazing teeth they are! Like the teeth of a serrated knife, a great white shark's teeth are jagged—the better to grab prey with slippery bodies. These weapons of mass destruction create wounds so deep that prey quickly bleeds to death, so a great white does not even have to put up a fight for its dinner.

With a sense of smell ten thousand times better than a human's, a great white shark can detect the presence of a single drop of blood dissolved in one million gallons of water.

THAT'S WILD!

10 WILD AND WILY

Some predators appear to be master planners. When it comes to capturing prey, here are ten animals that use their smarts in what appear to be extremely well thought-out strategies.

Where did I leave my car keys?

ARCTIC CAT

#9

Meerkat

While adult meerkats have some immunity to the stings of their favorite food, the scorpion's large pincers and stinging tail can still inflict plenty of damage. When hunting scorpions, meerkats have learned to quickly bite their prey's head or abdomen to disable them. Young pups, however, must learn this from their elders. The adults provide their young with scorpions in different stages of dismemberment to teach them exactly how it's done.

#10

Raven

Whoever coined the word *birdbrain* couldn't have known just how smart ravens are! When ravens that hide food know they are being watched, they do their best to fake out the observer, including checking false hiding places or trying to sneak away. Some ravens have learned to pull fishing lines toward them to check the ends for food. Such behaviors—being able to use deceit or to imagine outcomes—take sophisticated brains.

To learn more about meercats, watch *Meerkat Manor* on Animal Planet.

THAT'S WILD!

#8

Orb-web Spider

When spiders snare prey in their webs, they first disable the prey with a venomous bite. This saves the web from possible destruction while the prey struggles. The orb web spider, however, takes a different approach when it finds a bombardier beetle—an insect with the ability to shoot boiling hot liquid at enemies—caught in its web. It approaches the beetle gently, cautiously wrapping it in silk, without causing it to spray. When the spider does bite into its beetle dinner to liquefy its insides, the silk protects the spider against the full effects of the spray.

#7

Sabre-toothed Blenny

The cleaner wrasse is a fish that makes a living picking parasites off other fish. However, this friendly fish has an evil twin called the sabre-toothed blenny. Sporting the same stripes down its side as a cleaner wrasse and mimicking its movements, the sabre-toothed blenny has a mouthful of teeth like a miniature shark! Sidling up close to a client fish waiting to be cleaned, the blenny attacks and makes off with a mouthful of healthy flesh.

#6

Termite Assassin Bug

To raid a termite mound for its favorite meal, an assassin bug covers itself in pieces of termite plaster (the material used to build the mound) so it looks, feels, and smells just like part of the nest. Instead of attacking the bug as an intruder, the termites allow the stranger into the colony. The assassin bug then grabs a termite and uses its beak like a hypodermic needle to suck the life out of its helpless victim. Then it keeps hold of the dead termite to lure other termites, which always hurry to remove a dead body from the nest.

#5
Sea Otter

The sea otter may be the only marine mammal that has figured out how to use tools. The fact that abalone, the seafood it craves, comes in a very hard-to-open shell, was probably what inspired it to begin. When an otter finds an abalone, it hunts around until it finds rocks that it judges to be the perfect size and shape for specific tasks. It then lies on its back and, holding the food on its chest, uses one kind of rock to hammer the prey's shell open and another kind to pry it loose.

#4
Woodpecker Finch

The woodpecker finch, nesting on the Galapagos Islands, is one of Darwin's finches—a group of a dozen or so closely related birds that Charles Darwin observed. These observations helped him to develop his theories on evolution. The woodpecker finch has talents that include tool use as well as tool making. It makes up for its short tongue by grasping a cactus spine in its beak and using it to pry grubs out of branches. While it enjoys its grubby lunch, the finch holds the cactus spine in its claw to use again and again. Some birds have even been observed modifying the spines to make them easier to use.

They ran out of forks.

Egyptian Vulture

Equal in size to two-dozen chicken eggs, the ostrich egg is the largest on the planet, which is exactly why the egg-loving Egyptian vulture likes them. The trouble is, these eggs are really strong—a human adult can sit on one and it won't break—and the Egyptian vulture has a relatively weak beak and claws. Luckily for the vulture, it's not weak in the brain! All it has to do is find a suitable rock to get cracking. A vulture can wander over 130 feet in search of the perfect rock. Once the rock is firmly in its beak, the clever vulture whacks the egg with the rock. After a few tries, it is usually rewarded with an omelet.

Another name for the Egyptian vulture is "pharaoh's chicken."

THAT'S WILD!

One Western omelet coming right up!

#2 Green Heron

Green herons are experts at fishing. Most herons stand and wait for unsuspecting fish to swim near, but green herons go one step further: They make their own lures out of twigs or feathers. Besides fashioning homemade lures, these birds also have been observed using bait such as dead insects, earthworms, bits of Styrofoam, and crusts of bread they've retrieved from the garbage. After dropping the bait into the water, they play the waiting game at the water's edge. When a fish rises to the bait, the heron sees it right away. In a flash, it swoops down and snaps up a nice fish dinner. Tool use in green herons is rather uncommon. According to some researchers, only extremely intelligent individuals use the technique.

#1 chimpanzee

When it comes to using tools, chimps are the champs. No other animal turns as many different types of objects into tools, showing an amazing talent for creative problem solving. Chimps will strip branches of their leaves to use as "fishing" poles, then stick the branches into termite mounds to dip for the insects, which will clamp onto the sticks with their jaws. Chimps have also been recorded using a stick to break open the nesting chambers of hornbills to get at the fledglings, and they've been observed throwing stones at fruit to knock it down from trees. It turns out that different populations of chimps use different objects to make tools, and the parent chimpanzees teach their children these tool-making skills. Scientists say that this is the beginning of primitive culture.

SPECIAL REPORT:
Nutcrackers

Since panda nuts, one of a chimpanzee's favorite snacks, come wrapped in a tough shell, several bands of chimps have figured out how to get at the nut inside. First they carefully select stones with natural handles to use as hammers. Then they practice how to use them. If they hit too hard, the nut gets pulverized and if they don't hit hard enough, the shell won't crack. When they hit it just right, the prize stays intact. ●

11 HEAVY HITTERS

Predators come in all sizes, from microscopic bacteria to the largest mammal on Earth. But there's little doubt that the bigger and stronger the predator, the more impressive it is. Here are ten of the largest predators of their kind, whose size and power make them the ultimate in extreme killing machines.

#9

Harpy Eagle

The harpy eagle of Central and South America is the world's biggest and most powerful bird of prey. Females, which are larger than males, can reach 3.5 feet in length and weigh up to 20 pounds. Pity the prey that winds up in this eagle's talons, which are powerful enough to crush bones. A harpy eagle's 7-foot wingspan casts a monstrous shadow as it swoops through the rainforest to snatch its dinner—a monkey, a sloth, or even a deer!

#10

Goliath Birdeater Tarantula

Birds, mice, and frogs beware! That big hairy spider crawling on the ground just might eat you for dinner. With a weight of 2.5 ounces and a leg span of up to 11 inches, the Goliath birdeater tarantula is the world's largest spider. This fearsome killer attacks its prey, striking with its fangs and injecting venom. It then softens up its meal with digestive juices, mashes it into a pulp, and slurps up the liquid food.

#8

Komodo Dragon

Weighing as much as 300 pounds and reaching a length of 10 feet, the Komodo dragon is the largest lizard in the world. The Komodo dragon uses its sharp, jagged teeth to rip apart and devour almost anything. It will even ambush such huge prey as a 2,000-pound water buffalo. If by chance the prey escapes with only a bite, poisonous bacteria in the dragon's saliva ensure that the victim will die. All the dragon has to do is wait until it detects the smell of the decomposing body—which can be up to 7 miles away—and then head out to eat.

#7

Green Anaconda

Green anacondas are the world's heaviest snake, weighing up to 550 pounds. Anacondas are good swimmers and spend much of their time in swampy areas of South America. With their eyes and nostrils near the top of their head, anacondas can remain mostly submerged—making it easy for them to ambush thirsty prey. When these snakes strike, they sink their teeth in, coil themselves around their prey, and squeeze them to death.

Reticulated pythons, which can reach 33 feet, are generally considered to be the longest snake.

THAT'S WILD!

#6

Giant Squid

The giant squid is the largest invertebrate in the world, possibly growing as long as 100 feet. Up until recently, no one had ever seen a living giant squid in its natural habitat, and scientists figured that such huge creatures were probably sluggish hunters. Then in 2005, Japanese researchers dangled a camera 2,950 feet beneath the sea—and recorded a 26-foot-long female aggressively attacking the bait hanging below it.

The giant squid's eyes are as big as dinner plates.

THAT'S WILD!

#5

Amur Tiger

This is one kitty you don't want to scratch behind the ears! At up to 650 pounds and 13 feet long, the Amur, or Siberian, tiger is the largest tiger and the world's biggest cat. Given its size, you'd think it would be hard for an Amur tiger to sneak up on its prey. Not so! The striped pattern of its fur helps it go undetected in the forest where it lives, and the soft pads on the bottom of its paws ensure that prey will not hear it stalking them. And the tiger always hunts into the wind, so its prey can't get a whiff of its scent.

Every tiger has a different pattern of stripes, just as every person has different fingerprints.

THAT'S WILD!

My lips are SEALED!

SPECIAL REPORT: Endangered!

Because of their stunning fur and the use of virtually every part of their body in folk medicines, tigers have been hunted almost to extinction. Though it's now illegal, hunters continue to stalk and kill tigers for their body parts. One hundred years ago, there were roughly 100,000 tigers in the wild. Today, there are only about 5,000. •

#4

Polar Bear

Weighing in at up to 1,700 pounds and measuring about 10 feet long, the polar bear is the largest predator on land. It spends the winter months hunting on the sea ice in Arctic areas and south into Canada's Hudson Bay. Seals are this great white hunter's favorite food, but it will also eat just about anything else, from walruses weighing over a ton to human garbage. Even though it's a fast runner and an excellent swimmer, this powerful predator will often just hang out on the ice near a seal's breathing hole and ambush the animal when it pops up for a breath of air.

A polar bear's fur is actually transparent, not white.

THAT'S WILD!

Saltwater Crocodile

Found along the coasts of India, northern Australia, Indonesia, New Guinea, and Southeast Asia, saltwater crocodiles are the largest reptiles, weighing as much as 2,000 pounds and growing up to about 20 feet long. They are also extremely dangerous and will eat any kind of animal they come across, including humans.

Though saltwater crocodiles are capable of jumping straight up out of the water to capture birds and bats, they usually lurk beneath the surface with just their eyes and nostrils exposed. When a tasty-looking meal happens by, such as a water buffalo, a monkey, or a wild boar, they lunge at it and—*crunch*! One bite from the crocodile's powerful jaws is often enough to make the kill. When that doesn't work, it will drag its prey underwater until it drowns. A crocodile doesn't chew its prey but swallows it whole or, in the case of larger prey, in big chunks.

- Male saltwater crocodiles are about 17 years old and females are about 12 before they can breed. They are believed to live for about 50 years in the wild.
- Female saltwater crocodiles lay up to 70 eggs in large nest mounds built near rivers and streams.
- Saltwater crocodile embryos get oxygen through their eggshells. If the nest mound is flooded, the embryos will drown.

THAT'S WILD!

Elephant Seal

Elephant seal bulls sport a large inflatable trunk-like nose, making it easy to see how the animals got their name. During breeding season, bulls challenge each other with a mighty roar, and scientists think their nose may act like a trumpet to amplify the sound. The northern elephant seal bull has the longer schnozz, overhanging its mouth by 11 inches, while the southern elephant seal bull's only overhangs by about 4 inches. The male southern elephant seal, however, takes the prize for largest carnivore (meat eater), maxing out at more than 8,000 pounds.

Southern elephant seals are the diving stars of the ocean. Capable of diving several thousand feet, they can stay down for up to two hours at a time preying on squid and fish. They accomplish this remarkable feat by lowering their heart rate to a single beat per minute. No other sea mammal can dive as deep or stay underwater for as long—not even the whale.

Southern elephant seals congregate on land only twice a year, to breed and molt. Otherwise, they are solitary creatures, with males spending up to nine months and females up to ten months at sea—with about 90 percent of that time spent underwater hunting for prey!

From the south with a big mouth!

My shnozz is biggah than yours!

#1 Blue Whale

Blowing bubbles is fun!

Some scientists think that the blue whale is the largest mammal ever to inhabit the Earth. It certainly is the largest mammal living today. Females are larger than males, reaching a length of almost 100 feet and weighing more than 150 tons—about the weight of 25 adult male African elephants, which are the largest mammals on land.

You'd think such an enormous animal would require large prey. Quite the contrary! The blue whale feeds almost entirely on krill (tiny shrimp-like creatures), and lots of them. Every day it can eat as much as four tons of food—or around 40 million krill! All it has to do is open its cave-like mouth and take a huge gulp of krill-filled seawater. The pleated grooves in its throat expand to take it in. Then, as the whale closes its mouth, the throat contracts and forces the water back out through the hundreds of short, overlapping baleen plates that hang down from the whale's upper jaw, trapping the krill against the baleen. All that's left is for the whale to lick the krill off with its 4-ton tongue and take another gulp.

- The sounds made by a blue whale are much louder than a jet engine yet so low in frequency that humans can't hear them. The sounds can, however, be heard by another blue whale hundreds of miles away.
- A newborn blue whale calf is more than 20 feet long and can weigh up to 3 tons. Each day, it consumes about 50 gallons of its mother's high-fat milk and gains more than 200 pounds!

THAT'S WILD!

12 BLOODSUCKERS

Some of nature's tiniest creatures can turn out to be among the most extremely terrifying predators. Animals that suck the blood of their prey often spread diseases, many of which can paralyze and even kill their victims!

#10

Vampire Finch

The vampire finch uses its long, sharp beak to peck at the skin of seabirds called boobies until they bleed, and then the little vampire drinks their blood. Stranger still, scientists think the boobies allow this to happen because the pecking resembles their own grooming behavior. Perhaps that's why they're called boobies! During breeding season, the vampire finch supplements its bloody diet with booby eggs.

#9

Sea Lamprey

With rows of sharp teeth lining a sucker-like mouth that, when fully opened, is wider than its body, the sea lamprey is a fearsome killer of other fish. Once it fastens onto its prey, the lamprey uses its tongue to rip away scales and skin. It then secretes a substance that thins the blood, allowing it to feast on the fish's blood and body fluids until it's either had enough or the fish is dead. This eel-like ocean fish has also invaded the Great Lakes, where it's become a pest in some areas.

No,
it's not an
earring!

7

Conenose Bug

The conenose bug is also called the kissing bug because it often hovers around the lips of a sleeping person. First, it numbs the skin by injecting saliva filled with painkillers through its beak-like mouthparts. Then it slurps up the victim's blood. Conenose bugs, particularly in Latin America, sometimes carry a parasite that causes an illness known as Chagas' disease. The parasite is spread when feces from the bug get into a wound. Chagas' disease can affect the brain, digestive system, and heart and, if left untreated, it can be fatal.

#8

Candiru

Found in rivers, lakes, and streams, this South American freshwater fish swims back through the flow of water from a fish's gills, anchors itself inside the gill, and feeds on blood and body tissue. It's feared by swimmers because it will also follow the trail of blood or urine and lodge itself inside an injury or private passageway to feed. Once inside another body, the candiru is almost impossible to remove except through an operation.

#6

Vampire Bat

The common vampire bat is a stealth hunter that preys on cattle, horses, and other livestock. All this tiny predator needs is about one ounce of blood a night, and it prefers to lap its blood meal while its victim is sleeping. The bat has heat-sensitive pits on its face that help it pick an effective spot to bite. Then it uses its sharp teeth to make a shallow wound. Chemicals in its saliva keep the blood flowing while it licks up the fluid. Luckily for humans, the vampire bat prefers the blood of hoofed mammals to that of people.

#5

Mosquito

Did you know that only the female mosquito bites? It needs a nice long sip of mammal blood so its eggs can develop properly. Male mosquitoes mostly feed on nectar and plant juices. Female mosquitoes have beaks that are both pointed for piercing skin and hollow, like a straw, for sucking blood. Before starting to suck, the mosquito injects its victim with a substance to prevent the blood from clotting so that it will flow freely into the mosquito's mouth. That's the substance that causes the itch. It's also the substance that can spread terrible diseases, such as West Nile virus, encephalitis, yellow fever, and malaria. Mosquitoes can drink about 1.5 times their weight in blood.

Mosquito-borne illnesses have caused more human deaths than all the wars in history put together!

THAT'S WILD!

#4

Leech

A leech is a type of worm that likes nothing better than some warm mammal blood for dinner. Sensors on its head detect slight changes in light and air temperature—clues that tell the leech that an animal is nearby. Then the leech will slither toward its meal until, by trial and error, it makes contact. At that moment, the leech will bite and begin to suck. A leech can suck up to five times its body weight in just 20 minutes. Once it's full, it simply drops off and doesn't have to eat again for several months.

The Hirudo, or medicinal leech, has 32 brains! Doctors used to use it to cure everything from headaches to gout. Today, they are used in plastic and reconstructive surgery.

THAT'S WILD!

#3 Bedbug

A little creature that no one likes just might be sharing your nice warm bed with you. After years of keeping a low profile in the United States, bedbugs are making a comeback. They've popped up in the bedrooms of houses, hotels, apartments, and dormitories all over the land. A number of scientists who study bugs for a living had never even seen a live bedbug until recently. The reason? Fifty years ago, the pesky critters were wiped out by pesticides. Now it seems that foreign bedbugs are hitching rides in the suitcases of international travelers.

Bedbugs are attracted by carbon dioxide—the air that we humans and other animals breathe out. Bedbugs also crave warmth, which is why they end up sharing people's beds. Bedbugs can ingest up to seven times their weight in blood, visibly increasing their size after just one meal. Though a bedbug bite is extremely itchy, it's not usually dangerous. Some people, however, can develop an allergic reaction to bedbug saliva.

Flea

Fleas—what a nuisance! These tiny bloodsuckers cause a lot of itchy annoyance for their warm-blooded hosts by crawling around and biting them. The problem is that sometimes you're not just dealing with the flea—you are dealing with a germ that lives inside that flea. Such is the case with rat fleas that carry the bacterium *Yersinia pestis*, which causes bubonic plague, also called black plague.

Plague is primarily a disease of rats and other rodents. But when a rat host dies from plague infection, the tiny insect parasite that lives off the rat jumps to the next best (and often closest) available host: a person. And it takes the bacteria with it. The resulting infection is the disease that is responsible for periodically wiping out huge chunks of the world's population throughout history. Plague still infects wild animal populations today, but now that scientists understand the bacteria and the infection pattern better, it does not cause such huge and dangerous outbreaks.

Ticks—tiny arachnids no bigger than the head of a pin—only need to eat three times in their entire lives. But when they do eat, watch out! Hard ticks can drink up to 600 times their weight in blood. When they are through drinking, ticks can be as fat as marbles. Ticks are experts at finding hosts—animals that will provide them with their next liquid meal. Many people think that ticks jump up from the ground onto their victims. That's not what they do at all. Instead, the tick climbs to the top of a blade of grass or shrub and waits for a warm body to wander by. When a potential host nears, the tick raises its legs and wiggles them in the air; this is called questing behavior. If the host brushes past, the tick latches on. Ticks have the perfect mouthparts to get what they need—a straw-like pointed beak for plunging in and sucking. The hook on the end holds the tiny predator firmly in place. After ticks have drunk all the blood their bodies will hold, they drop off the host and molt, transforming to the next developmental stage. Ticks are major spreaders of Lyme disease, Rocky Mountain spotted fever, and many other serious illnesses. After hiking in the woods—or even messing around in your backyard—be careful to check yourself and your pets for ticks.

Some ticks release a mild painkiller when they bite so that a person might not know that a tick has latched on until it has fed.

THAT'S WILD!

77

Glossary

algae aquatic organisms similar to plants but lacking roots, stems, and leaves

ambush to hide and then attack without warning

antenna one of a pair of sensory appendages that serve as an organ of touch for insects and crustaceans

antivenin a substance that counteracts the effects of venom

arachnid an arthropod with four pairs of legs and a body divided into two parts; spiders, mites, and scorpions are arachnids

arthropod an animal with a segmented body and jointed, external skeleton that must be shed in order to grow; insects, spiders, crustaceans, and centipedes are all arthropods

bacteria simple one-celled microorganisms, some of which cause disease in humans and animals

baleen a stiff yet elastic substance found in the upper jaws of certain whales that is used to filter krill out of seawater

bioluminescence visible light produced by a chemical reaction inside certain organisms; fireflies and many deep-sea animals produce bioluminescent light

blubber a thick layer of fat found in many marine mammals

camouflage blending in with one's environment due to protective coloring

carcass a dead body

carnivore a predator that eats flesh

cartilage tough connective tissue that supports and anchors muscles

chelicerae an arachnid's fang-like appendages used for grasping and piercing

colony a group of the same type of organisms, which live together

echolocation a sensory system that allows the animals, such as bats and dolphins, to determine the direction and distance of objects based on echoes produced from their high-pitched cries

electroreception an animal's ability to receive and interpret electrical impulses

embryo the earliest stage of a developing organism

fovea a small part in the retina that is responsible for sharp vision

habitat the environment in which an animal is normally found

invertebrate an animal without a backbone

kelp a type of brown seaweed

krill tiny shrimp-like crustaceans

larva the early stage of metamorphosis in many insects, when they appear as wingless, often wormlike, creatures

mammal a warm-blooded animal with a backbone; female mammals give birth to live young and produce milk to nourish them; humans, apes, and whales are all mammals

mandible a jaw-like appendage near an insect's mouth

marsupial a mammal that is born prematurely and continues its development outside the womb; most marsupials are found in Australia and the Americas

mimicry when an organism develops over time to look or act like another organism in order to protect itself from predators

nocturnal being most active at night

nymph an early stage of metamorphosis in certain insects in which they resemble smaller, wingless versions of the adults they will become

parasite an animal that feeds and lives off another animal without contributing to the host animal's survival

pheromone a chemical secretion by a certain animals, especially insects, that is often used to attract mates

pinniped any flesh-eating mammal that lives in water and has a streamlined body and flippers; walruses and seals are pinnipeds

pod a group of marine mammals, such as dolphins or whales

predator an animal that hunts other animals for food

prey an animal hunted for food by another animal

proboscis a trunk or unusually large snout or nose; also the long, tubular feeding part of certain animals such as butterflies

radula a tongue-like organ found in the mouths of snails, slugs, and certain other mollusks

raft a group of penguins

savanna a flat, tropical or subtropical grassland, usually with scattered trees

species a category or class of animals that share certain characteristics; members of the same species can have offspring after mating

talon the claw of an animal, especially a bird of prey

urticating hairs barbed hairs that cover a New World tarantula's abdomen; some tarantulas flick the hairs at their enemies; if embedded, these hairs can cause irritation

venom a poisonous substance made by certain animals and delivered through a bite or a sting

wingspan the distance between the tips of an animal's wings

Resources to Find Out More

Books

Dangerous Animals, by John Siedensticker, Barnes & Noble Books, 2003

Killer Science: Nature's Deadliest Predators, by Shelly Silbering, McGraw-Hill, 1999

Nature's Predators, by Michael Bright, Robin Kerrod, and Barbara Taylor, Anness Publishing, Ltd., 2003

Web Sites

Animal Planet
http://animalplanet.com
Official Web site for Discovery Channel's Amimal Planet, featuring fan sites for favorite series, videos, pet guides, games, interactives and much more.

Food Chains and Webs
http://www.vtaide.com/png/foodchains.htm
Explains how a food chain works and allows you to create your own.

National Zoo: Just for Kids
http://nationalzoo.si.edu/Audiences/kids
Articles, stories, games, and activities on the world's animals, including predators.

Photo Credits

The editors wish to thank the following organizations and individuals for permission to reproduce the images in this book. Every effort has been made to obtain permission from the owners of all materials. Any errors that may have been made are unintentional and will be corrected in future printings if notice is given to the publisher.

T = Top; B = Bottom; C = Center; L = Left; R = Right

Index